A Teacher's Guide to
The Lion, the Witch and the Wardrobe

a novel by C. S. Lewis

by
Christin Ditchfield

Carson-Dellosa Publishing Company, Inc.
Greensboro, North Carolina

Table of Contents

CD-104149 A Teacher's Guide to *The Lion, the Witch and the Wardrobe*

Table of Contents

Meet the Author

Clive Staples Lewis was born on November 29, 1898, in Belfast, Northern Ireland. When he was four years old, he changed his name to "Jacksie" and refused to answer to anything else! Jack's older brother Warnie was his constant companion and closest friend. They spent countless hours exploring the forests and fields around their country home. On rainy days, they climbed up into an old wardrobe and told each other stories about knights and dragons, magic kingdoms, and talking animals that lived in faraway lands.

Jack was only nine when his mother, Flora, was diagnosed with cancer. He fervently prayed for a miracle, pleading with God to heal her. But Flora died, and Jack felt betrayed. He turned his back on God completely, dismissing religion and the teachings of the Christian church as foolishness.

During World War I, Jack was sent to the front lines in France, where he was wounded in battle. He returned home to complete his education, becoming a professor of medieval and Renaissance literature at Oxford. Lewis published several volumes of poetry and developed a reputation as a distinguished scholar and literary critic. About this time, he began engaging in heated intellectual debates with professors who were Christians, including fellow author J. R. R. Tolkien. These friends and coworkers challenged Lewis to rethink his beliefs. At the age of 31, after a lengthy struggle, the avowed atheist became a devout Christian.

Later Lewis wrote *Surprised by Joy*—a kind of spiritual autobiography that described his journey to faith. Then, books such as *Mere Christianity*, *The Problem of Pain*, and *The Screwtape Letters* brought Lewis worldwide fame. In the 1950s, Lewis wrote a series of seven books for children—including *The Lion, the Witch and the Wardrobe*—which he called *The Chronicles of Narnia*. Immediately best-sellers, Lewis's fairy tales are now widely regarded as "classic literature"—considered to be among the greatest children's books ever written.

Lewis had no children of his own. He remained a bachelor until the age of 58, when he met and married American writer Joy Davidman. When Joy died of cancer only four years later, Lewis looked after her two teenage sons. On November 22, 1963, the world was reeling over the assassination of President John F. Kennedy. In the light of that tragedy, Lewis's death from a long illness was barely noticed.

To date, C. S. Lewis's books have sold more than 200 million copies and have been translated into 30 languages. He is routinely quoted by preachers and professors, presidents and prime ministers. Many of the most prominent leaders of the Christian faith today readily acknowledge having been profoundly influenced by the man *Time* magazine called "a young atheist poet who became one of the 20th century's most imaginative theologians."

An Introduction to
The Lion, the Witch and the Wardrobe

A best-seller ever since its release in 1950, *The Lion, the Witch and the Wardrobe* has been called a classic fairy tale and a literary masterpiece. The adventure begins when Peter, Susan, Edmund, and Lucy tumble through the door of a mysterious wardrobe into Narnia, an enchanted world of talking beasts, fauns, dwarfs, and giants. The children discover that Narnia is in bondage—held captive under the spell of the evil White Witch. "It's she that makes it always winter; always winter, and never Christmas!" Prophecies have foretold the end of the Witch's reign. One day, the great Lion Aslan, King of Beasts, will return to Narnia. Furthermore, two "Sons of Adam" and two "Daughters of Eve" will sit on the four thrones at Cair Paravel and rule as Kings and Queens in Narnia. Now that the four children are here, could it be that Narnia's deliverance is at hand?

The Lion, the Witch and the Wardrobe is a story of redemption and the sacrifice that makes that redemption possible. In one sense, all of Narnia is waiting to be redeemed. The land itself longs to be free—to return to the peace, joy, and beauty it once knew. The story is also about personal redemption. When Edmund falls under the spell of the White Witch, he succumbs to pride, selfishness, and greed, betraying his brother and sisters. He becomes a traitor. And according to the Deep Magic (or law) on which Narnia was founded, he must pay the penalty with his life.

The only hope for Narnia and for Edmund is Aslan, the one who created Narnia. Only Aslan can deliver them from the power of the Witch. Aslan lays down his own life for Edmund, taking Edmund's punishment and dying in his place. Ultimately, it is in dying at the hands of the Witch that Aslan sets Narnia and Edmund free because there is an even "Deeper Magic"—a greater law—at work: "When a willing victim who had committed no treachery was killed in a traitor's stead, the Table would crack and Death itself would start working backward." With Aslan's sacrifice on the Stone Table, the power of the Witch's spell is broken. The eternal winter has ended; spring has come. Aslan's resurrection marks the dawn of the Golden Age of Narnia.

We hope you will enjoy using this workbook as you and your students begin your own adventures in the wonderful world of Narnia!

Using This Teacher's Guide

By taking advantage of students' tremendous interest in fantasy literature and providing them with some truly exciting, fun, and creative activities that build on the skills they may already have, *A Teacher's Guide to The Lion, the Witch and the Wardrobe* can assist you in maintaining student excitement for independent reading. It can also help you explore some of the many principles presented in the novel.

We recommend that you use the reproducible pages in ways most appropriate for your students and classroom setting. For example, some advanced students and older classes may be able to answer the comprehension questions in a test format, while others may need to tackle them in a group or with an open book. The questions could also be asked aloud as starting points for group discussions.

Vocabulary Words Begin by reading appropriate chapters in *The Lion, the Witch and the Wardrobe*. Then, have students use dictionaries to match the vocabulary words to the definitions provided. You may prefer to have older students look up and record the definition of each word themselves. In that case, simply cover the definitions on the right side of the page before copying and handing out to students.

Additional ways to use the vocabulary words:
- Have students keep a record of the different pages on which they find the words.
- Have a vocabulary bee. Let students try to either spell or define the words.
- Let students describe the context clues that helped them figure out the definitions.
- Look up words in different dictionaries and compare the definitions; compare the meanings of British words with their American or Canadian meanings.

Comprehension Questions These questions range from recounting simple facts to determining character motivation, foreshadowing, and consequences. They can be used as discussion starters, journal prompts, or homework assignments. They may also be used on tests or quizzes.

Making the Story Your Own These sections emphasize character development by encouraging students to evaluate the behaviors and choices of the characters in the story and then apply what they have learned to their own lives.

Other Activities As with the other sections in this book, the activities may be completed individually or in groups—aloud or on paper. Some activities lend themselves to group projects, while others are more suited for individual completion. Before completing any food activity, ask families' permission and inquire about students' food allergies and religious or other food preferences. Modify the activities in ways that seem most appropriate for your students. Have fun with them, and your students will, too!

Creating a Journal

Keeping a journal is a wonderful way for students to reflect on and respond to *The Lion, the Witch and the Wardrobe* in a personal way. They can record their responses to the activities in this teacher's guide, as well as their own thoughts and ideas, artwork, and poetry. A journal helps students keep their class work organized and encourages them to do even more writing on their own.

Making a Journal

- Fill a three-ring binder or three-pronged pocket folder with 50-100 pages of lined notebook paper. Or, simply bind the pages together with yarn, ribbon, rubber bands, or brass fasteners.

- Photocopy the journal title page (page 8) for students. Have them fill in and illustrate the cover.

- A reproducible journal entry page (page 9) is also provided. Depending on the size of the class and the number of journal entries you anticipate, you may want to provide just a few copies of this page, reserving it for special entries or assignments. You could also use the page for individual essays you wish to display in a student's portfolio or on a classroom bulletin board.

- If your students have access to the technology, you may allow them to create their journals on a computer— in a word processing file or on a class Web site. In place of original drawings, they can incorporate artistic fonts and clip art.

Using a Journal

- Suggest that students take notes as they read the novel. Have them record questions they may have or ideas that come to them.

- Have students answer the vocabulary and comprehension questions in their journals.

- Assign topics from the story, such as: "Father Christmas gave the children some rather unique gifts. What is the most unusual gift you have ever received?" or "If you could grow up to become a king or queen of Narnia, what would you like to be known for?"

- Remind students that they are welcome to include personal opinions and observations, such as how they feel about certain characters, whether they like how the story unfolds, or what they would do differently.

- Allow students to use different colored pens and pencils to illustrate their entries.

The Lion, the Witch and the Wardrobe

a novel by C. S. Lewis

A Journal By

_____

Date Begun

_____

Lucy Looks into a Wardrobe

Directions: Match the following vocabulary words with the correct definitions. If you're not sure, use a dictionary to look up the words you don't know.

1. _____ splendid
2. _____ row
3. _____ passages
4. _____ wireless
5. _____ looking-glass
6. _____ wardrobe
7. _____ blue-bottle
8. _____ inquisitive
9. _____ muffler
10. _____ parcels
11. _____ faun

a. a kind of housefly
b. a warm scarf
c. questioning or curious
d. a noisy argument
e. long hallways
f. packages
g. excellent
h. mirror
i. British word for radio
j. a tall piece of furniture used to store clothing
k. an imaginary goat-like creature in Greek mythology

Comprehension Questions: Answer in your journal or in the space provided.

1. Who are the four children in the story, and where have they been sent to stay?

_____

_____

2. How do the children plan to spend their first day? Why do they change their plans, and what do they do instead?

_____

_____

3. At what does Lucy decide to take a closer look?

_____

4. Why does Lucy take care to leave the door open?

_____

_____

5. What does Lucy see, and whom does she meet?

_____

Vocabulary and Comprehension

CD-104149 A Teacher's Guide to *The Lion, the Witch and the Wardrobe*

Lucy Looks into a Wardrobe

During World War II, German fighter planes conducted air raids against Great Britain. They dropped hundreds of bombs on the cities, including England's capital city, London. Whenever possible, British parents sent their children to live with friends and relatives out in the country where it was much safer. That's why, in *The Lion, the Witch and the Wardrobe*, the four children find themselves at the Professor's house.

To find out more about the time in which this story takes place, use the Internet, a dictionary, an encyclopedia, or a history book to answer the following questions:

1. When did World War II begin? _____   When did it end? _____

2. Which countries fought in the war?

    _____

    _____

3. Describe some of the causes of the war.

    _____

    _____

4. List some of the major battles or events.

    _____

    _____

5. Name some historical figures who played important roles in the war.

    _____

    _____

6. What was the outcome of the war?

    _____

    _____

What Lucy Found There

Directions: Match the following vocabulary words with the correct definitions. If you're not sure, use a dictionary to look up the words you don't know.

1. ____ melancholy
2. ____ nymphs
3. ____ dryads
4. ____ jollification
5. ____ handkerchief
6. ____ bawled
7. ____ innocent
8. ____ stole

a. parties and celebrations
b. very sad
c. harmless
d. shouted
e. fairy-like spirits who live in trees
f. female fairy-like spirits who live in forests, mountains, and streams
g. a small cloth used for wiping the face or blowing the nose
h. moved along quietly or secretly, as to escape (comes from the word "stealth")

Comprehension Questions: Answer in your journal or in the space provided.

1. Where does Lucy go with Mr. Tumnus and why?

_____

2. What plans does Mr. Tumnus have for Lucy?

_____

3. Why does he change his mind?

_____

4. Who is the White Witch? What spell has she cast over Narnia?

_____

5. What does Lucy give to Mr. Tumnus?

_____

Making the Story Your Own: Answer the following questions in your journal or on a separate piece of paper. To feel compassion means to care for someone who is suffering and to want to help him.

1. How does Mr. Tumnus show compassion for Lucy?
2. How does Lucy show compassion for Mr. Tumnus?
3. How have you shown compassion to others?
4. How have others shown compassion to you?

CD-104149 A Teacher's Guide to *The Lion, the Witch and the Wardrobe*

What Lucy Found There
Lucy's Adventures in Narnia

In Chapters One and Two, C. S. Lewis introduces us to several characters, including Lucy and Mr. Tumnus. When we analyze or study the characters in a story, we can make predictions about the characters and events in the story. It can be fun to make predictions and then compare our ideas to the actual events as the story unfolds.

Directions: Answer the following questions, using the information you find in Chapter Two. Look for clues in the story. Write your answers in your journal or on a separate piece of paper.

1. Why is Mr. Tumnus friendly to Lucy?

2. Why does Lucy accept his invitation?

3. What sort of creatures live in Narnia?

4. How does the weather or time of year in Narnia compare to that of England?

5. Who is Mr. Tumnus afraid of?

6. What makes Mr. Tumnus cry?

7. Why does Mr. Tumnus change his mind about following the Witch's orders?

8. What kind of person is Lucy?

9. How does the White Witch treat people who dare to disobey her?

10. Why do you think the White Witch wants to catch "Sons of Adam" and "Daughters of Eve"?

11. Will the White Witch find out that Mr. Tumnus let Lucy escape? If so, how?

12. What will happen when Lucy tells her brothers and sister about her adventure inside the wardrobe? What will the others say or do?

Afternoon Tea with Mr. Tumnus

When Mr. Tumnus meets Lucy in the forest, he invites her to tea. In England, "tea" is more than a hot drink. The word often refers to a light meal served between an early lunch and a late dinner, usually at 3 or 4 o'clock in the afternoon. Just for fun, invite your friends or classmates to join you for tea. If you want to, you can serve soft-boiled eggs and sardines on toast, as Mr. Tumnus did. Here are some other traditional and tasty treats your guests will enjoy:

- Small sandwiches—with the crusts removed—cut into triangles or squares
- A variety of cookies, cakes, scones, and fruit tarts

How to Make Tea

You will need one tea bag for each cup of water—usually 3–4 tea bags per teapot. You can use an ordinary black tea, such as "orange pekoe," or a flavored herb tea.

1. Bring cold water to a full boil, either in a kettle or a saucepan on the stove.
2. Ask an adult to help you pour the boiling water over the tea bags in a teapot.
3. Let the tea brew for 4-5 minutes.
4. Serve with lemon or milk and sugar.

English Scones

This delicious pastry is a cross between a cookie and a muffin. The recipe makes 10-12 scones.

Ingredients
  2 cups all-purpose flour
  $2/3$ cup granulated sugar
  1 stick (113 grams) butter
  $1/4$ cup shortening
  1 egg
  $1/2$ cup raisins

Ingredients for Step Four
  1 lightly beaten egg
  1 tablespoon sugar

Directions
1. Mix all ingredients together by hand. If they don't blend well, add a splash of milk.
2. Pat out dough to $1/2$" (1.3 cm) thickness. Cut into circles with a cookie cutter or jar lid.
3. Bake for 8-10 minutes at 400° F (204° C) on an ungreased cookie sheet.
4. Flip over scones, brush tops with beaten egg, and sprinkle with sugar. Bake another 8-10 minutes until lightly brown.
5. Allow the scones to cool completely. Serve plain or topped with butter.

CD-104149 A Teacher's Guide to *The Lion, the Witch and the Wardrobe*

Edmund and the Wardrobe

Directions: Match the following vocabulary words with the correct definitions. If you're not sure, use a dictionary to look up the words you don't know.

1. _____ batty   **a.** miserable or awful
2. _____ hoax   **b.** a call for peace to end a fight
3. _____ spiteful   **c.** strict or harsh
4. _____ bathing   **d.** covered with a fine layer of gold
5. _____ heather   **e.** crazy
6. _____ wretched   **f.** mean or nasty
7. _____ pax   **g.** a trick or practical joke
8. _____ sledge   **h.** British word for swimming
9. _____ gilded   **i.** bushes with tiny pink or purple flowers
10. _____ stern   **j.** a sled or sleigh usually pulled by horses or other animals

Comprehension Questions: Answer in your journal or in the space provided.

1. How do Peter, Susan, and Edmund react to Lucy's story about the world inside the wardrobe?

   _____

2. Why won't Lucy do as they say and admit that her story isn't true?

   _____

3. What makes Lucy climb into the wardrobe again?

   _____

4. Why does Edmund follow Lucy into the wardrobe?

   _____

5. Who does Edmund meet in Narnia?

   _____

Edmund and the Wardrobe
The Queen of Narnia

As Edmund stands there in the forest, he hears the sound of bells . . .
and then a sledge appears, carrying a most unusual-looking woman.

A **descriptive paragraph** tells about something, such as a person, place, or thing. A descriptive paragraph should allow the reader to see, hear, smell, taste, and feel the things being described. Good descriptions help readers imagine what it's like to be in the story.

1. Reread the section in Chapter Three where Edmund meets the mysterious woman on the sledge. List the words and phrases that the author uses to describe this woman and her companions:

"The Queen"	The Dwarf	The Sledge
_____	_____	_____
_____	_____	_____
_____	_____	_____
_____	_____	_____
_____	_____	_____
_____	_____	_____

2. Using the author's descriptions and your own imagination, draw in your journal your own picture of what Edmund saw—the "Queen of Narnia" on her sledge.

3. In your journal, write a paragraph that describes what the Queen saw when she looked at Edmund. Describe the place where she found him, what he was doing, how he seemed to look and feel. Reread the chapter for clues to help you. Fill in the details with your own imagination.

Descriptive Paragraphs

CD-104149 A Teacher's Guide to *The Lion, the Witch and the Wardrobe*

Turkish Delight

Directions: Match the following vocabulary words with the correct definitions. If you're not sure, use a dictionary to look up the words you don't know.

1. _____ dominions
2. _____ mantle
3. _____ relations
4. _____ courtiers
5. _____ nobles
6. _____ flushed
7. _____ naiads

a. important people of wealth and high rank
b. turned red with embarrassment or discomfort
c. attendants in a royal court
d. fairy-like spirits that live in lakes, rivers, springs, and fountains
e. a loose robe, cloak, or cape
f. large areas of land controlled by a single ruler
g. members of one's family

Comprehension Questions: Answer in your journal or in the space provided.

1. What does Edmund ask the Queen to give him?

   _____

2. How does the Queen discover that Lucy has been to Narnia and met the Faun already?

   _____

3. What question does the Queen ask over and over again?

   _____

4. What does the Queen promise Edmund if he will bring his brother and sisters to her?

   _____

5. What does Lucy tell Edmund about the Queen?

   _____

Making the Story Your Own: Answer the following questions in your journal or on a separate piece of paper.

1. Why should Edmund be on his guard with the Queen?

2. Are people always what they seem?

3. Edmund lets greed get the better of him. Why is giving in to greed dangerous?

Turkish Delight

Edmund discovers that there are two very different ways to see the Lady he has just made friends with—the way she describes herself and the way others describe her. As you read through Chapter Four, make a note of the similarities and differences. Fill in the separate ovals below. In the middle, write those things on which everyone agrees. Here are some questions to get you started:

- What does the Lady call herself? What do others call her?
- What does she look like?
- What is her job or position?
- What abilities does she have?
- What kind of person is she? How does she treat people?
- How does she feel about children—"Sons of Adam" and "Daughters of Eve"?

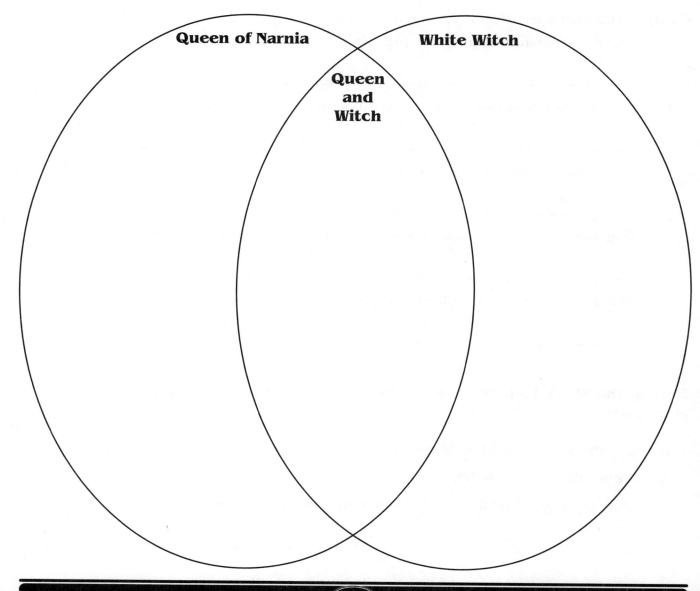

Queen of Narnia

White Witch

Queen
and
Witch

Compare and Contrast

CD-104149 A Teacher's Guide to *The Lion, the Witch and the Wardrobe*

Edmund's Turkish Delight

When the Witch offered Edmund anything he wanted to eat, he chose Turkish Delight—a gooey kind of sugar-coated fruit-flavored candy very popular in England and other European countries. If you'd like to try it, ask an adult to help you with this recipe. Unlike the enchanted kind, this candy is only delicious—not dangerous!

Ingredients

2 cups granulated sugar
1 1/4 cups water
1 lemon (peel cut into strips,
    the juice squeezed and strained)
1 orange (peel cut into strips,
    the juice squeezed and strained)
4 tablespoons unflavored powdered gelatin
1 tablespoon cornstarch
2 tablespoons powdered sugar

Directions

1. Dissolve the granulated sugar in the water in a saucepan on medium heat.
2. Add the strips of lemon and orange peel and the juices. Bring to a boil and simmer for 15 minutes.
3. Soak the gelatin in the mixture for 5-10 minutes. Strain into a shallow pan or platter. Let it set for 24 hours.
4. Cut the candy into 1" (2.54 cm) squares.
5. Sift the cornstarch and powdered sugar together in a shallow dish. Roll the pieces of candy into the mixture and serve.
6. Store the candies on waxed paper with the extra cornstarch and powdered sugar mixture. Keep loosely covered.

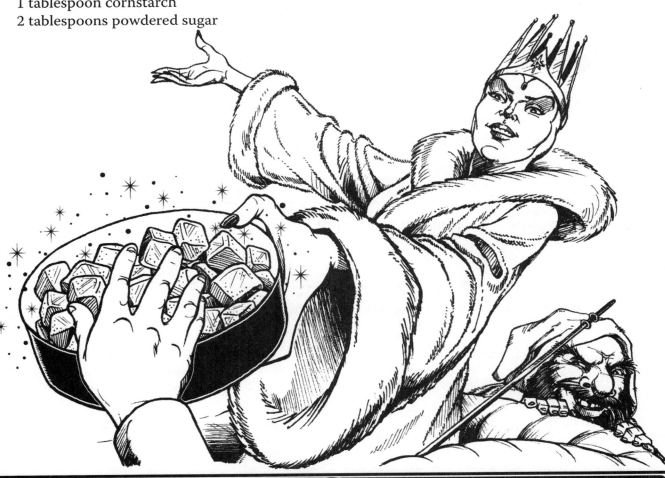

Back on This Side of the Door

Directions: Match the following vocabulary words with the correct definitions. If you're not sure, use a dictionary to look up the words you don't know.

1. _____ sulky
2. _____ superior
3. _____ taken aback
4. _____ at one's disposal
5. _____ reliable
6. _____ logic
7. _____ spectacles
8. _____ trippers

a. surprised
b. eyeglasses
c. angry and silent
d. better than others
e. available as needed
f. British word for tourists
g. trustworthy or dependable
h. careful and correct thinking

Comprehension Questions: Answer in your journal or in the space provided.

1. What does Edmund tell the others about his and Lucy's adventures in Narnia?

   _____

2. Why do Peter and Susan decide to talk things over with the Professor?

   _____

3. What does the Professor give as the "three possibilities"?

   _____

4. What reasons does the Professor give for believing Lucy?

   _____

5. How do all four children end up climbing into the wardrobe?

   _____

   _____

Back on This Side of the Door
Peter, Susan, Edmund, and Lucy

The Professor tells Peter and Susan that one way to determine whether someone is telling the truth is to carefully consider what you know about her character—what kind of person she is. Looking back on what has taken place in the story so far, list words that describe what you know about each of the four children.

Peter	Susan
_____	_____
_____	_____
_____	_____

Edmund	Lucy
_____	_____
_____	_____
_____	_____

In the space provided below, answer the following questions:

1. Of the four children, who would you trust and why?

    _____

    _____

2. Who would you most like to have as a friend? Why?

    _____

    _____

Into the Forest

Directions: Match the following vocabulary words with the correct definitions. If you're not sure, use a dictionary to look up the words you don't know.

1. _____ camphor
2. _____ bagged
3. _____ prigs
4. _____ charred
5. _____ crockery
6. _____ treason
7. _____ chatelaine
8. _____ fraternizing
9. _____ enchantment
10. _____ horrid
11. _____ larder

a. a pantry or place where food is stored
b. a magic spell
c. partly burned
d. a female ruler; a woman of power and authority
e. being friendly with
f. pottery dishes
g. turning against your own country and assisting its enemies
h. stolen
i. awful
j. a substance made of tree bark that keeps moths and insects away
k. people whose manners are too perfect; irritatingly proper

Comprehension Questions: Answer in your journal or in the space provided.

1. What does Peter do as soon as he realizes that Narnia really does exist?

_____

2. How does Edmund let it slip that he really has been to Narnia before?

_____

3. What has happened to Mr. Tumnus?

_____

4. What do the children decide to do about Mr. Tumnus and why?

_____

5. What creature suddenly appears in the forest? What does it want the children to do?

_____

CD-104149 A Teacher's Guide to *The Lion, the Witch and the Wardrobe*

Into the Forest
Have a Debate

As the children begin their adventures together, they are forced to make some difficult decisions:

    🌶 Should they try to rescue Mr. Tumnus or just go home?

    🌶 Should they follow the robin deeper into the forest or not?

Peter, Susan, and Lucy want to help Mr. Tumnus, but Edmund thinks there is nothing they can do. Lucy wants to follow the robin, but Susan isn't sure. Edmund says that the robin may be leading them into a trap. What do you think?

Have a Debate A debate is a contest in which two opposing sides of a position are argued by two or more speakers.

1. Form debate teams of four or five people. Choose one of the two topics listed above.

2. Create a position statement. Your statement tells if you will be arguing that the children should or should not try to help Mr. Tumnus (or that the children should or should not follow the robin). You may have to argue a position with which you disagree.

3. Research the issue. With your team, look for places in the text that support your position. Be prepared to quote them during the debate. Also think of other places you can research to help your argument. For instance, what about Peter's remark that robins are always "good birds" in other stories? Can you find examples of stories that feature robins as good birds?

4. Brainstorm as a team to identify three or more important arguments that will support your position.

5. List your arguments in descending order of importance. In other words, list the most important argument first, then the next-most-important argument second, etc. Prepare a conclusion that summarizes the most important points.

6. Select a member of your team who you feel will best present your arguments and state your team's conclusion. Help the presenter practice a five-minute speech. Use a watch or timer to ensure that the time limit is met.

7. Extend your debate by including a question-and-answer session. Give each member on both teams an opportunity to ask one question of an opposing team member. Limit answers to one minute.

8. Conclude your debate and determine a winner. Let the audience of the debate vote and then give feedback as to why the winning team was more persuasive.

CD-104149 A Teacher's Guide to *The Lion, the Witch and the Wardrobe*

Into the Forests of Narnia

Help the Pevensie children find their way through the woods to the Beavers' dam.

A Day with the Beavers

Directions: Match the following vocabulary words with the correct definitions. If you're not sure, use a dictionary to look up the words you don't know.

1. _____ beckoned   **a.** shovels
2. _____ earnestly   **b.** branches
3. _____ boughs   **c.** a piece or part of a song
4. _____ token   **d.** cooking stove
5. _____ strain   **e.** seriously
6. _____ trifle   **f.** a sign or symbol
7. _____ festoons   **g.** not very valuable or important
8. _____ oilskins   **h.** jam made from oranges
9. _____ spades   **i.** flowers, ribbons, and other decorations
10. _____ trowels   **j.** waterproof coats and pants
11. _____ range   **k.** tools with flat blades used for laying cement
12. _____ marmalade   **l.** gave a signal or gesture to ask someone to come closer

Comprehension Questions: Answer in your journal or in the space provided.

1. How does Mr. Beaver prove to the children that he is a friend?

_____

2. Describe how each of the four children responds to the mention of Aslan's name.

_____

3. Where does Mr. Beaver take the children?

_____

4. What does Edmund see in the distance, and what does it make him think of?

_____

5. What does Mrs. Beaver say that shows that she has been expecting the children and that she is very excited about their arrival?

_____

A Day with the Beavers
Telling the Story

Authors carefully choose descriptive words to help readers get to know the characters in a story and give readers a way to picture the scenes in their heads. There are many descriptive words and phrases in Chapter Seven. Create your own list, using the guidelines below. Focus on the words that give you the most information—the ones that help you imagine how the characters and settings look or feel.

A **noun** is the name of a person, place, or thing. An **adjective** describes something or somebody. An **adverb** tells how something is done and usually ends in "ly."

List adjectives that describe the Beavers.

_____

_____

_____

List adjectives that describe the river.

_____

_____

_____

List adjectives that describe the Beavers' dam—inside and out.

_____

_____

_____

List some things (nouns) in or around the forest, the river, and the Beavers' dam.

_____

_____

_____

List the adverbs that describe any action that takes place in Chapter Seven.

_____

_____

_____

Another way to describe something is to compare it to something else— often using the words "like" or "as." List some examples from Chapter Seven.

_____

_____

_____

Parts of Speech

CD-104149 A Teacher's Guide to *The Lion, the Witch and the Wardrobe*

What Happened After Dinner

Directions: Match the following vocabulary words with the correct definitions. If you're not sure, use a dictionary to look up the words you don't know.

1. _____ stratagem   **a.** people who travel from place to place to sell things
2. _____ peddlers   **b.** a demon or genie
3. _____ Jinn   **c.** not to be trusted; dangerous or tricky
4. _____ prophecy   **d.** turned against someone and caused him great harm
5. _____ betrayed   **e.** a clever plan
6. _____ treacherous   **f.** a prediction or saying about something that will happen in the future

Comprehension Questions: Answer in your journal or in the space provided.

1. Who is Aslan?

_____

2. Where does Mr. Beaver say he will take the children? Why?

_____

3. Why does the White Witch want to capture and kill any "Sons of Adam" or "Daughters of Eve"?

_____

4. How does Mr. Beaver know where Edmund has gone?

_____

5. Who or what is the only hope for Mr. Tumnus, the children, and Narnia itself? Why?

_____

_____

 © Carson-Dellosa   Vocabulary and Comprehension

What Happened After Dinner

After dinner, Mr. and Mrs. Beaver tell the children about Aslan—Narnia's true king. Go back through Chapter Eight and see if you can answer the questions below. Answer in your journal or in the space provided.

1. List some of the different names or titles Mr. Beaver uses for Aslan.

   _____

2. What kind of creature is Aslan?

   _____

3. How do most people feel when they first meet Aslan?

   _____

4. Mr. Beaver says of Aslan: "'Course he isn't safe. But he's good." What do you think Mr. Beaver means by that?

   _____

5. Read the prophecies below. According to Mr. and Mrs. Beaver, what do the Narnians believe the prophecies mean? Answer in your journal.

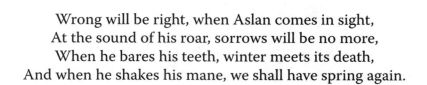

Wrong will be right, when Aslan comes in sight,
At the sound of his roar, sorrows will be no more,
When he bares his teeth, winter meets its death,
And when he shakes his mane, we shall have spring again.

When Adam's flesh and Adam's bone
Sits at Cair Paravel in throne,
The evil time will be over and done.

CD-104149 A Teacher's Guide to *The Lion, the Witch and the Wardrobe*

What Happened After Dinner
Adam's Flesh and Adam's Bone

Mr. Beaver recites several prophecies in the form of rhymes or poems that promise better days for Narnia and its creatures. Reread the poems in Chapter Eight. Then, write a poem of your own in your journal or on a separate piece of paper. Your poem could be about a particular character, such as Peter, Aslan, or the White Witch. It could be about an event, such as Lucy's first adventure in the wardrobe or the arrest of Mr. Tumnus. It could describe a particular place in Narnia. Or, your poem could express your feelings about the story. When you have decided what you will write about, consider what type of poem you would like to write.

Free verse is poetry without any rules of form, rhyme, or rhythm.

A **limerick** is a short, humorous poem with five lines. Lines one, two, and five rhyme with each other, while lines three and four rhyme with each other. There are three stressed syllables in lines one, two, and five. There are two stressed syllables in lines three and four. (Stressed syllables are read with special emphasis.)

> *There once was a Witch who was White*
> *Who made magic Turkish Delight.*
> *With a drop in the snow,*
> *She could make a box grow,*
> *And you'd wish you could eat it all night.*

A **ballad** is a type of poem that tells a story. Each stanza has four lines. Many times the second and fourth lines rhyme. In the example below, each line contains a rhyme within itself.

Wrong will be right, when Aslan comes in sight,
At the sound of his roar, sorrows will be no more,
When he bares his teeth, winter meets its death,
And when he shakes his mane, we shall have spring again.

In the Witch's House

Directions: Match the following vocabulary words with the correct definitions. If you're not sure, use a dictionary to look up the words you don't know.

1. _____ give the cold shoulder
2. _____ reckoned
3. _____ shins
4. _____ cinema
5. _____ schemes
6. _____ sorcerer
7. _____ turret
8. _____ ventured
9. _____ satyrs
10. _____ centaur
11. _____ eerie

a. a round tower on a castle
b. movie theater
c. did something risky or dangerous
d. plans or plots
e. horse- or goat-like creature in Greek mythology
f. thought
g. strange or frightening
h. parts of the legs between the knees and the ankles
i. to be uncaring toward someone on purpose
j. a magician or wizard
k. a creature with the head, arms, and chest of a man and the body of a horse

Comprehension Questions: Answer in your journal or in the space provided.

1. Why does Edmund sneak out of the Beavers' dam? Where does he go?

   _____

2. What thoughts keep Edmund from turning back?

   _____

3. What sight terrifies Edmund when he first enters the courtyard?

   _____

4. Who is Maugrim?

   _____

5. Why is the White Witch angry with Edmund when he arrives?

   _____

Vocabulary and Comprehension

CD-104149 A Teacher's Guide to The Lion, the Witch and the Wardrobe

In the Witch's House
A Creepy Courtyard

The **mood** of a book is the overall feeling a reader gets while reading. Mood usually changes throughout the story. An author creates a mood by using descriptive words that make the reader feel a certain way. The story setting and story events also help to develop the mood.

Use the chart below to describe the mood in this chapter. Look for nouns and adjectives the author uses to help create the mood. (Remember that a **noun** is a person, place, or thing and an **adjective** is a word that describes a noun.)

Event	Feelings Associated with the Event	Adjectives or Phrases Used by the Author
1. Edmund listens to the conversation about Aslan.		
2. Edmund discovers that the Witch's "house" is really a castle.		
3. Edmund realizes the lion in the courtyard is a statue.		
4. Maugrim takes Edmund to the Witch.		
5. Edmund tells the Witch his news.		

Optional Activities:

- In your journal or on a separate piece of paper, write a paragraph in which you compare and contrast the mood of this chapter with the mood of the previous chapter.

- Test your own writing skills. Try to create a certain mood as you write a paragraph of your own. Remember to use adjectives to make it calm and peaceful, tense and suspenseful, mysterious and scary, or happy and hopeful.

CD-104149 A Teacher's Guide to *The Lion, the Witch and the Wardrobe*

Mood

The Spell Begins to Break

Directions: Match the following vocabulary words with the correct definitions. If you're not sure, use a dictionary to look up the words you don't know.

1. _____ crock
2. _____ plaguey
3. _____ flask
4. _____ frowsty
5. _____ solemn
6. _____ sluice gate
7. _____ sheath
8. _____ quiver
9. _____ cordial

a. a carrying case for arrows
b. pottery container
c. stale, musty, or damp
d. a medicine you drink
e. small flat bottle
f. serious
g. a holder for a knife, dagger, or sword
h. device that controls the flow of water in a channel or dam
i. troublesome, irritating, or annoying

Comprehension Questions: Answer in your journal or in the space provided.

1. Why do Mr. Beaver and the children get impatient with Mrs. Beaver?

_____

2. Where do the travelers stop to spend the night?

_____

3. What noise frightens the children and why?

_____

4. Who has come to Narnia at last?

_____

5. What gifts does he bring?

_____

Making the Story Your Own: Answer the following questions in a journal or on a separate piece of paper. The children are given gifts that will help them fulfill their calling and face the challenges that lie ahead. What special gifts or talents have you been given? What character traits do you have that help you face life's challenges?

CD-104149 A Teacher's Guide to *The Lion, the Witch and the Wardrobe*

The Spell Begins to Break
What Will Happen Next?

Logic is a way of thinking in order to come to a conclusion or solve a problem. If you can make several true statements about something based on information you already have, you may be able to draw a conclusion or discover new information as a result.

For example: Mr. Tumnus is a faun.
                     All fauns have tails.
                     Mr. Tumnus has a tail.

See the connection from one statement to another? This is called a **logical syllogism**. If the statements are not connected, a wrong conclusion may be drawn.

Directions: Read the statements below. Write *yes* if the statements form a logical syllogism. Write *no* if the statements do not form a logical syllogism.

1. The Witch hates and fears the children.
    The Witch knows where the children are.
    The Witch will try to capture the children.

    _____

2. A spell kept Father Christmas out of Narnia.
    Father Christmas has come to Narnia.
    The spell has been broken.

    _____

3. Only Aslan can save the children.
    Aslan is at the Stone Table.
    Aslan is the king of Narnia.

    _____

4. Father Christmas has gifts for the children.
    The children have gifts for the Beavers.
    The gifts are "tools, not toys."

    _____

Challenge: In your journal, write a new logical conclusion for each set of statements you thought was not logical. Then, write two logical syllogisms of your own. Choose any topics you like.

Name: _____   Date: _____

Father Christmas Comes at Last

Unscramble the words below to find the gifts that Father Christmas gave the children.
Use the numbers to answer the question at the bottom of the page.

LDHIES   ___ ___ ___ ___ ___ ___
      7   13

DWORS   ___ ___ ___ ___ ___
         4

WBO   ___ ___ ___

EVIQUR   ___ ___ ___ ___ ___ ___

RRAWOS   ___ ___ ___ ___ ___ ___
            14

GAGRDE   ___ ___ ___ ___ ___ ___
      9 10   3

INDMODA   ___ ___ ___ ___ ___ ___ ___
         8

TBTOEL   ___ ___ ___ ___ ___ ___

AILORDC   ___ ___ ___ ___ ___ ___ ___
    6   5

OYIVR NRHO   ___ ___ ___ ___ ___ ___ ___ ___ ___
      15   2   12

RAAFKESTB   ___ ___ ___ ___ ___ ___ ___ ___ ___
          11   1

What wonderful news does Father Christmas bring?

"___ ___ ___ ___ ___ ___ ___ ___ ___
 9 7 13 9 12   5 7   14 12

___ ___ ___ ___ ___ ___ ___ .
1 2 3   8 14 15 3
,

___ ___ ___ ___ ___ ___ ___ ___ ___ ___ ___ ___ ___ ___ ___
1 2 3   4 5 1 6 2 7   8 9 10 5 6
"

___ ___ ___ ___ ___ ___ ___ ___ ___ ___ ___ .
5 7   4 3 9 11 3 12 5 12 10

Just for Fun

CD-104149 A Teacher's Guide to *The Lion, the Witch and the Wardrobe*

Chapter -11-

Aslan Is Nearer

Directions: Match the following vocabulary words with the correct definitions. If you're not sure, **use** a dictionary to look up the words you don't know.

1. _____ repulsive
2. _____ vermin
3. _____ gluttony
4. _____ traitor
5. _____ councillor/counselor
6. _____ snowdrops
7. _____ vicious
8. _____ crocuses
9. _____ laburnums
10. _____ transparent

a. mean and cruel
b. something so clear that it can be seen through
c. disgusting
d. greed, especially for food
e. bushes with bright yellow flowers
f. small animals that are harmful (like rats, fleas, lice)
g. long tube-like flowers
h. herbs with white flowers
i. someone who gives advice or suggestions
j. someone who is unfaithful and turns against his own friends, family, or country

Comprehension Questions: Answer in your journal or in the space provided.

1. What happens when Edmund asks the Witch for the Turkish Delight she promised?

_____

2. What is Maugrim ordered to do?

_____

3. Who do the travelers meet in the forest? What happens to them?

_____

4. Does the Witch treat Edmund like a Prince? Explain:

_____

5. What signs reveal that the Witch's spell has been broken?

_____

_____

Aslan Is Nearer
Then and Now

As the story unfolds, we learn more about each of the characters. Use the following chart to help you analyze and understand changes in the characters' behavior.

Review Chapters 4-6:

CHARACTER	ATTITUDE TOWARD EDMUND	EXAMPLES FROM STORY
THE WHITE WITCH		
PETER		
EDMUND HIMSELF		

Review Chapters 8-11:

CHARACTER	ATTITUDE TOWARD EDMUND	EXAMPLES FROM STORY
THE WHITE WITCH		
PETER		
EDMUND HIMSELF		

Optional Activity:

In your journal or on a separate piece of paper, describe how Edmund's attitude has changed toward the White Witch. What events or circumstances have caused the change to occur?

CD-104149 A Teacher's Guide to *The Lion, the Witch and the Wardrobe*

Peter's First Battle

Directions: Match the following vocabulary words with the correct definitions. If you're not sure, use a dictionary to look up the words you don't know.

1. _____ glades   **a.** difficult or embarrassing
2. _____ pavilion   **b.** rearing upon its hind legs
3. _____ rampant   **c.** killer
4. _____ standard   **d.** a large, and often beautiful, tent
5. _____ awkward   **e.** thick growth of bushes, shrubs, and trees
6. _____ thickets   **f.** open grassy spaces in the middle of a forest
7. _____ bane   **g.** the personal flag of a member of the royal family

Comprehension Questions: Answer in your journal or in the space provided.

1. How do the children feel about meeting Aslan for the first time?

   _____

2. What does Aslan say about saving Edmund?

   _____

3. What special responsibility will Peter have at Cair Paravel? Why?

   _____

4. What sound interrupts Peter's conversation with Aslan? What does it mean?

   _____

5. How does Peter "win his spurs"?

   _____

Making the Story Your Own: Answer the following questions in your journal or on a separate piece of paper. Has there ever been a time when you had to do something you were afraid to do? What was it? How did you find the courage to face your fears? How has that experience helped you face other challenges later on?

CD-104149 A Teacher's Guide to *The Lion, the Witch and the Wardrobe*

Vocabulary and Comprehension

Peter's First Battle
A Knight's Tale

After Peter proves himself in battle, Aslan makes him a knight of the realm and gives him the title "Sir Peter Wolf's Bane."

Using the Internet, an encyclopedia, or a book about medieval history, research the history and customs of knighthood. Prepare your report on a separate piece of paper. Here are some questions to get you started:

✒ During what period in history did the custom of knighthood begin?

✒ What types of achievements or qualifications did a person need in order to become a knight?

✒ Describe some of the rituals or ceremonies associated with knighthood.

✒ Name some famous knights from both history and legend.

A knight's shield was decorated with his "coat of arms"—a design made of colors and symbols that represented his achievements, his family background, or his country of origin. Research what kinds of symbols were used and what they represented. Then, try designing your very own "coat of arms" in the space provided below.

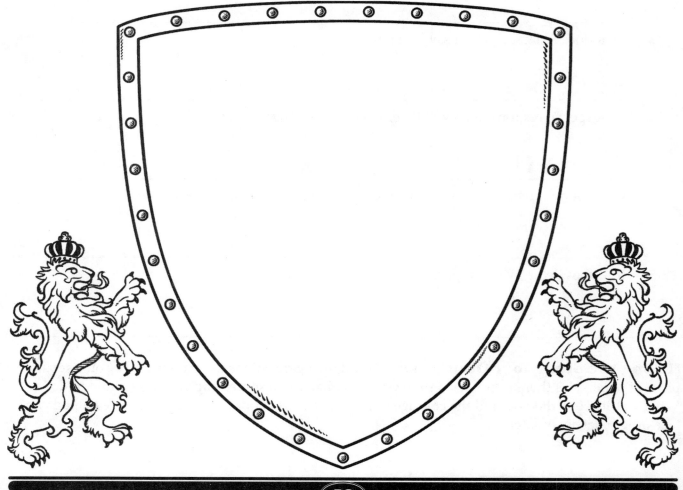

Research and Report

CD-104149 A Teacher's Guide to *The Lion, the Witch and the Wardrobe*

Deep Magic from the Dawn of Time

Directions: Match the following vocabulary words with the correct definitions. If you're not sure, use a dictionary to look up the words you don't know.

1.	_____ scornfully	**a.**	a rough, violent person; a beast
2.	_____ brute	**b.**	formal meeting
3.	_____ bound	**c.**	to lose the right to something
4.	_____ craves	**d.**	a higher, sharper sound
5.	_____ audience	**e.**	rod or staff carried by ruler
6.	_____ dispute	**f.**	tied up
7.	_____ shriller	**g.**	given up, rejected, or refused
8.	_____ scepter	**h.**	disagree or argue
9.	_____ forfeit	**i.**	to be destroyed
10.	_____ perish	**j.**	wants something desperately
11.	_____ renounced	**k.**	with hate or contempt; looking down on someone

Comprehension Questions: Answer in your journal or in the space provided.

1. What does the Witch decide to do to Edmund? Why?

   _____

2. What keeps the Witch from carrying out her plan?

   _____

3. Who sends a messenger to ask permission to speak with Aslan?

   _____

4. What is the Deep Magic? Who created it? What does it mean for Edmund?

   _____

5. What will happen to Narnia if the Law is not kept?

   _____

Chapter 13

Deep Magic from the Dawn of Time

Read the following quotes from Chapter Thirteen and paraphrase them. Put them into your own words and explain what they mean to the story.

1. Aslan says of Edmund, "Here is your brother . . . and there is no need to talk to him about what is past."

_____

_____

2. Aslan says of the Queen, "All names will soon be restored to their proper owners."

_____

_____

3. Mr. Beaver says to the Witch, "So that's how you came to imagine yourself a queen—because you were the Emperor's hangman."

_____

_____

4. The Witch says, "Unless I have blood as the Law says all Narnia will be overturned and perish in fire and water."

_____

_____

5. Aslan tells the children, "I have settled the matter. She has renounced the claim on your brother's blood."

_____

_____

_____

Comprehension

CD-104149 A Teacher's Guide to *The Lion, the Witch and the Wardrobe*

Deep Magic from the Dawn of Time
Magic at Work

To comprehend a story more clearly, it is important to realize why things happen. The events of a story can be organized and understood by cause and effect. The cause is the reason why something happens and the effect is the result, or what happens. Sometimes you may not be able to determine the cause and effect until you read more of the story.

Directions: Fill in either the missing cause or effect.

Cause	Effect
	The Witch decides to go ahead and kill Edmund in the forest.
The rescue party arrives just in time.	
	Edmund apologizes to his brother and sisters for betraying them.
The White Witch requests an audience with Aslan.	
The Deep Magic says that the Witch has the right to kill traitors.	
	For Narnia to survive, the Law must be kept.
Aslan has promised to do everything that can be done to save Edmund.	

  Cause and Effect

The Triumph of the Witch

Directions: Match the following vocabulary words with the correct definitions. If you're not sure, use a dictionary to look up the words you don't know.

1. _____ campaign
2. _____ siege
3. _____ muzzle
4. _____ rabble
5. _____ hoist
6. _____ whet
7. _____ pact
8. _____ appeased

a. a cover for an animal's mouth to keep it from biting
b. an agreement
c. surrounding a castle to cut off supplies and wait for surrender
d. to sharpen against a stone
e. a noisy crowd
f. to lift something heavy
g. battle plan
h. given what is needed; made calm or content

Comprehension Questions: Answer in your journal or in the space provided.

1. What does Aslan discuss with Peter and why?

_____

2. Why can't Susan and Lucy sleep?

_____

3. What arrangement has Aslan made with the White Witch?

_____

4. How do the Witch's creatures torment Aslan?

_____

5. What does the Witch tell Aslan right before she kills him?

_____

Making the Story Your Own: Answer the following questions in your journal or on a separate piece of paper. To sacrifice means to give up something important or enjoyable for a good reason. What does Aslan sacrifice for Edmund? Have you ever made a sacrifice—big or small—for someone else? Has anyone in your life ever made a sacrifice for you?

CD-104149 A Teacher's Guide to *The Lion, the Witch and the Wardrobe*

The Triumph of the Witch
Heroes and Villains

Classification is sorting people, places, or things into categories for specific reasons. Many different creatures are mentioned in *The Lion, the Witch and the Wardrobe*. Some of them are good, and some of them are evil. Go back through the chapters you've read so far—paying special attention to Chapters 12-14—and list the villains and heroes. Start with the characters who have names, then include types of creatures (such as fauns, wraiths, etc.).

Villains	Heroes
_____	_____
_____	_____
_____	_____
_____	_____
_____	_____
_____	_____
_____	_____
_____	_____
_____	_____
_____	_____
_____	_____
_____	_____

Deeper Magic from Before the Dawn of Time

Directions: Match the following vocabulary words with the correct definitions. If you're not sure, use a dictionary to look up the words you don't know.

1. ____ skirl
2. ____ vile
3. ____ incantation
4. ____ mount
5. ____ battlements

a. evil
b. an animal used for riding
c. a high, shrill, screaming sound
d. magic spell that is spoken or sung
e. the walls along the top of a castle that protect soldiers in battle

Comprehension Questions: Answer in your journal or in the space provided.

1. What does the White Witch do as soon as Aslan is dead?

_____

2. What do the mice try to do for Aslan?

_____

3. What sound do Susan and Lucy hear? What has happened?

_____

4. What is the Deeper Magic that the Witch did not know?

_____

5. Where does Aslan take Susan and Lucy?

_____

Making the Story Your Own: Answer the following questions in your journal or on a separate piece of paper. Make a list of the characters in this chapter who show courage and compassion. How do they demonstrate these qualities? In what ways could you practice courage and compassion in your life?

CD-104149 A Teacher's Guide to The Lion, the Witch and the Wardrobe

Deeper Magic from Before the Dawn of Time

Chapter Fifteen begins with great sadness: Aslan is dead. The chapter ends with great joy: Aslan is alive again! Go back through the chapter and look for the words and phrases that set the tone or mood. These nouns, adjectives, and verbs really help the reader feel the emotion. List them below.

Fear and Sadness   **Joy and Celebration**

_____   _____

_____   _____

_____   _____

_____   _____

_____   _____

_____   _____

A Deeper Magic from Before the Dawn of Time

ACROSS

3. He will defend Narnia in Aslan's absence.
5. The traitor condemned to die
9. This starts working backward
10. Emperor's Hangman
11. When Aslan comes to Narnia, the snow _____.
12. The only one who can save Edmund and Narnia
14. He put the Magic into Narnia when he created it.
15. What Aslan makes for Edmund
17. The sound of Aslan's victory
18. She witnesses Aslan's resurrection.
19. Aslan lays down his _____ for Edmund.

DOWN

1. "When he shakes his _____, we shall have spring again."
2. Where justice takes place
4. The reason for Aslan's sacrifice
6. The Law on which Narnia was founded
7. She comforts Aslan when he is sad and lonely.
8. King of Beasts
9. The Law the Witch did not know
13. They try to set Aslan free.
16. The sound of the Witch's defeat

     Just for Fun

CD-104149 A Teacher's Guide to *The Lion, the Witch and the Wardrobe*

What Happened about the Statues

Directions: Match the following vocabulary words with the correct definitions. If you're not sure, use a dictionary to look up the words you don't know.

1. _____ prodigious
2. _____ concealed
3. _____ interior
4. _____ ransacking
5. _____ liberated
6. _____ saccharine tablet
7. _____ din

a. the inside of something
b. set free
c. searching wildly for something
d. hidden
e. noise
f. huge, enormous
g. a sugar-like sweetener the size of an aspirin

Comprehension Questions: Answer in your journal or in the space provided.

1. Why has Aslan come to the White Witch's castle?

   _____

2. How does Aslan bring the statues back to life?

   _____

3. List some of the creatures who are rescued.

   _____

4. How is the battle going when Aslan and his army arrive? Why?

   _____

5. Who crushes the White Witch on the battlefield?

   _____

Making the Story Your Own: Answer the following questions in your journal or on a separate piece of paper.

1. When the battle began, Peter's army was desperately outnumbered. Do you think they were tempted to give up? What made them keep fighting? How was their perseverance rewarded?

2. When you face a challenging situation are you ever tempted to give up? How can you find strength to persevere?

What Happened about the Statues

Chapter Sixteen is made up of many different moments—individual encounters—between Aslan and the creatures who have been held captive in the Witch's castle.

Directions: On a separate piece of paper, write a summary of the things that take place in this chapter. A summary presents the most important ideas in a story or chapter, without all of the details. Use the following guide to help you with the writing process:

Prewriting (This is the planning stage. Do this before you write your summary.)

- Read the chapter carefully.
- Skim through it a second time, making a list of important ideas or events.
- Share your list with a partner to make sure you haven't missed anything.
- Make sure your ideas are in logical order. If not, number them to make writing easier.

Writing Your First Draft

- Your first sentence should be the topic sentence, which states the main idea of your summary.
- Remember to include only the most important information. Do not include many details.
- Add a concluding sentence if you think one is necessary.

Revising (Change ideas, add or remove sentences, evaluate your word choices.)

- Read your summary carefully to see if all of your important ideas are included.
- Make sure that you used your own words and use quotation marks for any quoted text.
- Check to make sure your sentences are interesting and that the summary you have written is thorough and doesn't leave out any major events.

Editing (Check carefully for errors. You might want to have a dictionary handy.)

- Check for spelling and punctuation errors.
- Trade papers with an editing partner.

Preparing a Final Draft

- Write the final draft of your summary in your best handwriting.

CD-104149 A Teacher's Guide to *The Lion, the Witch and the Wardrobe*

The Hunting of the White Stag

Directions: Match the following vocabulary words with the correct definitions. If you're not sure, use a dictionary to look up the words you don't know.

1. _____ revelry   **a.** friends, partners, or companions
2. _____ remnant   **b.** an animal that is being hunted
3. _____ alliance   **c.** fat or heavy
4. _____ valiant   **d.** celebration
5. _____ stout   **e.** brave and courageous
6. _____ consorts   **f.** friendly agreement to work together
7. _____ quarry   **g.** a message given by signs or symbols
8. _____ foreboding   **h.** a piece or part of something left over
9. _____ signification   **i.** the way you get from one place to another
10. _____ route   **j.** an inner sense that something bad is about to happen

Comprehension Questions: Answer in your journal or in the space provided.

1. What act of heroism does Edmund perform on the battlefield?

2. How does Lucy use the present Father Christmas gave her?

3. What do the children do for Narnia as Kings and Queens?

4. How do the children change over time? Who do they become?

5. How do the children end up back in the Professor's house?

Making the Story Your Own: Answer the following questions in your journal or on a separate piece of paper. Why does Lucy get angry with Aslan? Do you understand why she feels the way she does? What causes Lucy to apologize for her behavior? Was it the right thing to do?

Vocabulary and Comprehension

The Hunting of the White Stag
The Story Ends

Now that you have finished reading *The Lion, the Witch and the Wardrobe*, do you have any questions that were left unanswered? Write those questions here:

_____

_____

_____

_____

Is there anything about the story that you would change? Anything you wish had happened differently? Why or why not?

_____

_____

_____

_____

_____

On your own or in a small group, come up with your answers to the questions above and the ones listed below. When you finish brainstorming, share your thoughts with the class.

- Do you think Edmund should be told what Aslan has done for him?
- Is the White Witch really dead or just gone for now?
- Will the White Stag ever be caught? How? By whom?
- Who will rule Narnia now that the children are back in England?
- Will Aslan return to Narnia again?
- Will Peter, Susan, Edmund, and Lucy ever return to Narnia?
- What does the phrase, "Once a King in Narnia, Always a King in Narnia," mean?
- If the children do get to Narnia again, how will it happen?
- Will the children meet others who have been to Narnia?
- Will their adventures in Narnia change the way the children live in their own world? If so, how?

CD-104149 A Teacher's Guide to *The Lion, the Witch and the Wardrobe*

Once a King in Narnia, Always a King in Narnia

Find these people, places, and things from *The Lion, the Witch and the Wardrobe*. Answers can be found across, down, and diagonally.

Aslan

Beavers

Cair Paravel

Dwarf

Edmund

Father Christmas

King

Lucy

Magic

Mr. Tumnus

Narnia

Peter

Professor

Queen

Spring

Stone Table

Susan

Turkish Delight

Wand

Wardrobe

White Stag

Winter

Witch

Wolf

```
C Q E G I S E K I N G W T A W V E F V
U G B K J U U X O E T H P V I O Q A S
J J E K G S Q E W S Q I P W T U P T P
T A A I I A X N X E Y T E O C E R H R
A P V L H N A G L C Q E G L H T O E I
Q Z E J U L U B L U D S W F B N F R N
I R R N S C A C A D H T I L K A E C G
A R S A S T Y L A F B A S O I M S H O
E Z F R E W K O U I V G T B W A S R P
B L M N Z C A W M E R V C F A G O I D
U I O I S O S R B R E P K R N I R S E
V T T A V D E V D Q T X A W D C C T W
S L D K B W Z D P R F U O R Q O R M I
T X T P U A Q D M O O J M K A E C A N
M Y A K B R Y U J U L B T N T V J S T
Q U M R G F C P E R N V E E U Q E V E
A J O A E M P B A E Z D P N K S T L R
M N Q L G G B G W K N A Q A J T A P V
M T U R K I S H D E L I G H T M I H N
```

The Lion, the Witch and the Wardrobe

Matching: Match these words with the correct definitions.

1. _____ enchantment   **a.** predictions or sayings about the future
2. _____ prophecy   **b.** one who turns against his own friends, family, or country
3. _____ traitor   **c.** to set free
4. _____ forfeit   **d.** a magic spell
5. _____ liberate   **e.** to give up or surrender

True or False: Write *T* next to each true statement and *F* next to each false statement. On a separate piece of paper, explain why each false answer is false.

1. _____ Lucy discovers the world of Narnia when she climbs into a wardrobe.
2. _____ Edmund is a kind and caring brother to Lucy.
3. _____ The woman who calls herself "Queen of Narnia" is really a wicked witch.
4. _____ The Beavers are in the pay of the White Witch.
5. _____ The Deep Magic says the White Witch cannot kill anyone.
6. _____ There is a Deeper Magic that the White Witch doesn't know.
7. _____ Edmund is killed by the Witch on the Stone Table.
8. _____ When Aslan breathes on them, the stone statues come back to life.
9. _____ The White Witch escapes in the end.
10. _____ The four Pevensie children become kings and queens in Narnia.

Short Answer:

1. What spell has the White Witch cast over all Narnia?
2. Whose arrival signals the end of the Witch's reign?
3. What crime has Edmund committed?
4. Who leads the four children to Aslan?
5. How does Aslan satisfy the Witch's demand for Edmund's blood?

Essay:

Choose one of these two topics and write your essay on a separate piece of paper.

1. Describe Narnia when Lucy first discovers it and how it changes when Aslan appears.
2. Describe Edmund's character at the beginning of the story and compare it to his character at the end. Explain how his behavior changes and why.

Bonus Question:

What was your favorite part of the story? Why?

CD-104149 A Teacher's Guide to *The Lion, the Witch and the Wardrobe*

Book Report Ideas

There are many ways to do a report on a book you have just read. After you have finished *The Lion, the Witch and the Wardrobe*, choose one of the following projects or come up with one of your own!

- Design a book jacket with the title, author's name, and your own illustration on the front. On the inside left flap, write a description of the book. On the inside right flap, tell about the author.

- Write a letter to a friend, as if you are one of the main characters. Tell her the story as if it happened to you.

- Give it some careful thought, then make a list of the "Top Ten" reasons why everyone should read this book!

- Choose an important scene from the book and ask a few classmates to act it out with you. Use props and costumes if you want to or just use your imagination. Practice several times on your own, then perform the scene for the class.

- Draw a map of Narnia. Trace the journeys of the main characters or mark the locations where important things took place.

- Write a collection of three to five poems inspired by characters or events in the book.

- Create a time line of important events in the story. Describe each event in a few sentences.

- Pretend you are one of the main characters. Create a costume and come up with a list of questions about the character that you can answer. Ask your teacher or another student to "interview" you in front of the class.

- Make a model of an object from the story, such as the wardrobe, the Witch's house, the Beavers' dam, or the castle of Cair Paravel. Or, create a diorama of an important scene from the book.

- Design a series of seven bookmarks, each one featuring a specific person, place, or thing from the book. On the front, draw a picture of the subject. On the back, write a description that explains its importance to the story.

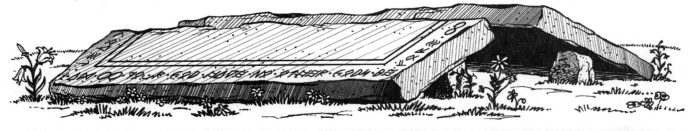

Recommended Resources

Other Books in The Chronicles of Narnia by C. S. Lewis

> Book One: *The Magician's Nephew*
> Book Three: *The Horse and His Boy*
> Book Four: *Prince Caspian*
> Book Five: *The Voyage of the Dawn Treader*
> Book Six: *The Silver Chair*
> Book Seven: *The Last Battle*

The Lion, the Witch and the Wardrobe was the first book C. S. Lewis wrote about Narnia. Later, he wrote six more, including a prequel explaining how Narnia came to be. At Lewis's suggestion, publishers renumbered the series to reflect the chronological order of the stories, rather than the publication dates.

Books about The Chronicles of Narnia

> Ditchfield, Christin. *A Family Guide to Narnia: Biblical Truths in C. S. Lewis's The Chronicles of Narnia.* Wheaton, IL: Crossway Books, 2003.
>
> Ford, Paul F. *Companion to Narnia.* San Francisco: HarperCollins, 1994.
>
> Gresham, Douglas. *The Narnia Cookbook.* San Francisco: HarperCollins, 1998.
>
> Riordan, James. *A Book Of Narnians.* San Francisco: HarperTrophy, 1997.
>
> Sibley, Brian. *The Land of Narnia.* San Francisco: HarperCollins, 1989.

Great Web Sites for Teachers and Students

> The Official Site of The Chronicles of Narnia
> www.narnia.com
>
> Explore the Breathtaking Fantasy World of
> C. S. Lewis on the Web
> www.virtualnarnia.com
>
> The C. S. Lewis Foundation
> www.cslewis.org
>
> The HarperCollins C. S. Lewis Site
> www.cslewisclassics.com

Answer Key

Page 10: Vocabulary and Comprehension

Vocabulary:	Comprehension:
1. g	1. Peter, Susan, Edmund, and Lucy come to stay at the Professor's house in the English countryside.
2. d	
3. e	2. They plan to explore the outdoors, but because of rainy weather, they end up exploring the house instead.
4. i	
5. h	3. Lucy opens the door of a large wardrobe.
6. j	4. It would be foolish to risk getting locked inside.
7. a	5. Lucy finds herself in a snowy wood. She sees a lamp-post in the middle of the forest and meets a faun who's carrying packages and an umbrella.
8. c	
9. b	
10. f	
11. k	

Page 11: Research and Report

1. 1939-1945
2. Allies—Great Britain, United States, France, British Commonwealths (Canada, Australia, New Zealand, etc.); Axis Powers—Germany, Italy, Japan
3. Aggression toward or invasion of other countries by Germany, Russia, Italy, and Japan
4. Answers will vary; examples may include Pearl Harbor, D-Day, etc.
5. Answers will vary; examples may include Churchill, Roosevelt, Hitler, Stalin, Mussolini, famous generals, or other war heroes.
6. The Allies were victorious.

Page 12: Vocabulary and Comprehension

Vocabulary:	Comprehension:
1. b	1. Mr. Tumnus invites Lucy to his cave for tea.
2. f	2. He was going to lull Lucy to sleep and turn her over to the Witch.
3. e	3. He discovers what humans are like and realizes it would be wrong.
4. a	4. She's an evil witch who makes it "always winter and never Christmas."
5. g	5. Lucy gives Mr. Tumnus her handkerchief.
6. d	
7. c	
8. h	

Making the Story Your Own:

1. Mr. Tumnus releases Lucy and helps her find her way home.
2. Lucy forgives Mr. Tumnus and comforts him.
3.-4. Answers will vary.

Page 13: Making Predictions (Answers will vary.)

Page 15: Vocabulary and Comprehension

Vocabulary:
1. e
2. g
3. f
4. h
5. i
6. a
7. b
8. j
9. d
10. c

Comprehension:
1. They don't believe Lucy. They think she's pretending or playing a joke.
2. Her story is true, and Lucy can't bring herself to tell a lie.
3. She is playing hide-and-seek with the other children, hears footsteps in the hall, and thinks she will be caught.
4. He wants to keep teasing her about her "imaginary country."
5. Edmund meets a woman on a sledge who calls herself "Queen of Narnia."

Page 16: Descriptive Paragraphs (Answers will vary.)

Page 17: Vocabulary and Comprehension

Vocabulary:
1. f
2. e
3. g
4. c
5. a
6. b
7. d

Comprehension:
1. He asks for Turkish Delight.
2. Edmund tells her the story.
3. The Queen asks how many brothers and sisters Edmund has.
4. She will make him a prince and give him rooms full of Turkish Delight.
5. Lucy has been to see Mr. Tumnus. She tells Edmund that the woman who calls herself Queen is really the White Witch.

Making the Story Your Own:
Answers will vary.

Page 18: Compare and Contrast (Answers will vary.)
Some examples:

Queen of Narnia	**Queen and Witch**	**White Witch**
kind, generous	drives a sledge	cruel, wicked
cares for people	carries a wand	tortures people
loves children	wears a crown	kidnaps children
patient, understanding	has magic powers	angry, impatient

Page 20: Vocabulary and Comprehension

Vocabulary:
1. c
2. d
3. a
4. e
5. g
6. h
7. b
8. f

Comprehension:
1. He lies and says that they were just pretending.
2. They are worried that Lucy is losing her mind.
3. Lucy is telling lies. Lucy is mad. Lucy is telling the truth.
4. Lucy has always been truthful in the past, and it's unlikely that she would have thought of the idea of the time difference.
5. They are hiding from Mrs. Macready, the housekeeper.

CD-104149 *A Teacher's Guide to The Lion, the Witch and the Wardrobe*

Page 21: Character Analysis (Answers will vary.)

Page 22: Vocabulary and Comprehension

Vocabulary:
1. j
2. h
3. k
4. c
5. f
6. g
7. d
8. e
9. b
10. i
11. a

Comprehension:
1. He apologizes to Lucy.
2. Edmund suggests that they head for the lamp-post.
3. Mr. Tumnus has been arrested by the secret police.
4. They decide to try to rescue Mr. Tumnus since he's in trouble for being kind to Lucy.
5. A robin signals to the children to follow him through the forest.

Page 24: Maze

Page 25: Vocabulary and Comprehension

Vocabulary:
1. l
2. e
3. b
4. f
5. c
6. g
7. i
8. j
9. a
10. k
11. d
12. h

Comprehension:
1. He shows them Lucy's handkerchief, given to him by Mr. Tumnus.
2. Edmund felt a mysterious horror; Peter felt brave and adventurous; Susan felt as if a delicious smell or strain of music floated by; Lucy felt like the holidays had just begun.
3. Mr. Beaver took them to his dam, across the river.
4. Edmund sees the hills where the Witch's palace is located, and it makes him think of Turkish Delight.
5. "So you've come at last! To think that ever I should live to see this day!"

Page 26: Parts of Speech (Answers will vary.)

Page 27: Vocabulary and Comprehension

Vocabulary:
1. e
2. a
3. b
4. f
5. d
6. c

Comprehension:
1. King of Beasts, King of Narnia, Lord of the Wood, Son of the Great Emperor-beyond-the-Sea
2. He will take them to the Stone Table to meet Aslan.
3. When the four thrones at Cair Paravel are filled by human kings and queens, it will mean the end of the Witch's reign—and her life.
4. He could see that Edmund had eaten the Witch's food. There was something treacherous in his face—a strange look in his eyes.
5. Aslan is the only hope because only he can defeat the White Witch.

Page 28: Comprehension
1. King of Beasts, King of Narnia, Lord of the Wood, Son of the Great Emperor-beyond-the-Sea
2. A great Lion
3. Nervous, scared, frightened
4. The King of Narnia isn't someone who can be controlled or manipulated or even always understood. But, he can be trusted.
5. Aslan will set Narnia free from the Witch's spell. When human beings, such as the four children, reign at Cair Paravel, the Witch will die.

Page 30: Vocabulary and Comprehension

Vocabulary:
1. i
2. f
3. h
4. b
5. d
6. j
7. a
8. c
9. e
10. k
11. g

Comprehension:
1. Edmund wants more Turkish Delight, so he goes to meet the Witch.
2. He thinks of what he will do when he is King of Narnia.
3. Edmund is frightened by a stone statue of a crouching lion.
4. Maugrim is a gray wolf who is Chief of the Witch's Secret Police.
5. She's angry that Edmund did not bring his brother and sisters.

CD-104149 A Teacher's Guide to *The Lion, the Witch and the Wardrobe*

Page 31: Mood (Answers will vary.)

Event	Feelings Associated with the Event	Adjectives or Phrases Used by the Author
1. Edmund listens to the conversation about Aslan.	fear, confusion	"mysterious and horrible"
2. Edmund discovers that the Witch's "house" is really a castle.	small, alone, frightened	"huge," "great," "strange," "knees knocking together, teeth chattering," "nearly made his heart stop beating"
3. Edmund realizes the lion in the courtyard is a statue.	happiness, relief, confidence, power	"relief," "warm all over," "lovely," "gloating," "childish," "jeering"
4. Maugrim takes Edmund to the Witch.	fear, worry, regret	"aching with cold," "heart-pounding," "trembling," "terrible," "sad"
5. Edmund tells the Witch his news.	excitement, enthusiasm, hope	"rushing eagerly forward," "tell her all he had heard"

Page 32: Vocabulary and Comprehension

Vocabulary:
1. b
2. i
3. e
4. c
5. f
6. h
7. g
8. a
9. d

Comprehension:
1. She insists on taking time to prepare food and supplies for their journey.
2. They climb into a hole or "hiding-place for beavers in bad times."
3. They hear jingling bells and think that the Witch has found them.
4. Father Christmas has come.
5. Mrs. Beaver—"a new and better sewing machine"
   Mr. Beaver—dam finished and mended, leaks stopped, new sluice-gate
   Peter—shield and sword
   Susan—bow with quiver of arrows and ivory horn
   Lucy—bottle of cordial and dagger
   All—five cups and saucers, sugar, cream, teapot with hot tea

Making the Story Your Own:
Answers will vary.

Page 33: Logic
   1.-2. yes
   3.-4. no

Page 34: Cryptogram Solution

Shield
Sword
Bow
Quiver
Arrows
Dagger

Diamond
Bottle
Cordial
Ivory Horn
Breakfast

Answer: "Aslan is on the move. The Witch's magic is weakening."

CD-104149 A Teacher's Guide to *The Lion, the Witch and the Wardrobe*

Page 35: Vocabulary and Comprehension

Vocabulary:

1. c
2. f
3. d
4. j
5. i
6. h
7. a
8. g
9. e
10. b

Comprehension:

1. She gives him dry bread and water.
2. He must go to the Beavers' dam and kill whatever he finds there.
3. They meet a party of forest creatures celebrating Christmas. The Witch turns them all into stone.
4. No. She treats him like a prisoner; starving him, beating him, tying him up.
5. Snow is melting, flowers are growing, birds are singing. Spring has come.

Page 36: Character Analysis (Answers will vary.)

Review Chapters 4-6:

CHARACTER	ATTITUDE TOWARD EDMUND	EXAMPLES FROM STORY
THE WHITE WITCH	kind, caring, interested in his welfare, promises to make him a Prince	calls him "poor child," offers him candy
PETER	angry, annoyed, irritated	tells him to leave Lucy alone, calls him a "poisonous little beast"
EDMUND HIMSELF	proud, powerful, confident, clever	smug, "superior," rude to the others

Review Chapters 8-11:

CHARACTER	ATTITUDE TOWARD EDMUND	EXAMPLES FROM STORY
THE WHITE WITCH	mean, angry, impatient, cruel	strikes him, yells at him, ties him up
PETER	worried, anxious, forgiving	"he is our brother," "he's only a kid"
EDMUND HIMSELF	sorry for himself, scared, lonely	"miserable," "sorry"

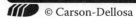 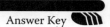
CD-104149 A Teacher's Guide to *The Lion, the Witch and the Wardrobe*

Page 37: Vocabulary and Comprehension

Vocabulary:	**Comprehension:**

Vocabulary:
1. f
2. d
3. b
4. g
5. a
6. e
7. c

Comprehension:
1. At first they're frightened and fidgety, then glad and peaceful.
2. "All shall be done. But it may be harder than you think."
3. Because he is firstborn, Peter will be High King over the others.
4. Susan has blown her horn to call for help. She's being attacked.
5. Peter saves Susan by killing the gray wolf.

Making the Story Your Own:
Answers will vary.

Page 39: Vocabulary and Comprehension

Vocabulary:
1. k
2. a
3. f
4. j
5. b
6. h
7. d
8. e
9. c
10. i
11. g

Comprehension:
1. She will kill Edmund to keep the prophecy from being fulfilled.
2. Aslan's creatures rescue Edmund and bring him to the Stone Table.
3. The White Witch wants permission to speak to Aslan.
4. The Emperor created the Deep Magic or Law on which Narnia is founded.
   The Law says that the Witch has the right to execute all traitors, including Edmund.
5. Narnia will be overturned and perish in fire and water.

Page 40: Comprehension (Answers will vary.)

Page 41: Cause and Effect

Cause: The Witch is afraid Edmund may escape.
Effect: The Witch decides to go ahead and kill Edmund in the forest.

Cause: The rescue party arrives just in time.
Effect: Edmund is rescued and taken to meet Aslan.

Cause: Aslan has a long talk with Edmund.
Effect: Edmund apologizes to his brother and sisters for betraying them.

Cause: The White Witch requests an audience with Aslan.
Effect: Aslan gives the Witch permission to come into the camp.

Cause: The Deep Magic says that the Witch has the right to kill traitors.
Effect: The Witch has the right to kill Edmund.

Cause: If the Law is not kept, Narnia will be destroyed.
Effect: For Narnia to survive, the Law must be kept.

Cause: Aslan has promised to do everything that can be done to save Edmund.
Effect: Aslan and the Witch talk alone.

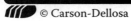 © Carson-Dellosa

Answer Key

Page 42: Vocabulary and Comprehension

Vocabulary:	Comprehension:

Vocabulary:
1. g
2. c
3. a
4. e
5. f
6. d
7. b
8. h

Comprehension:
1. They discuss a plan of attack against the Witch in case Aslan can't be there.
2. They have a feeling something is going to happen to Aslan.
3. He will take Edmund's place.
4. They shave him, muzzle him, kick him, spit on him, mock him.
5. His sacrifice was for nothing. She will kill Edmund anyway and rule all of Narnia.

Making the Story Your Own:

Answers will vary.

Page 43: Classification (Answers will vary.)

Page 44: Vocabulary and Comprehension

Vocabulary:
1. c
2. a
3. d
4. b
5. e

Comprehension:
1. She sets out to attack the children and the creatures of Narnia.
2. They try to set him free by nibbling away at the ropes that bind him.
3. They hear a deafening noise as the Stone Table cracks in two.
4. "When a willing victim who had committed no treachery was killed in a traitor's stead, the Table would crack and Death itself would start working backward."
5. He takes them on a wild ride across Narnia to the Witch's House.

Making the Story Your Own:

Aslan lays down his life for Edmund. Susan and Lucy keep Aslan company and experience his ordeal with him. The mice nibble through the ropes to set Aslan free. Other answers will vary.

Page 45: Vocabulary

Answers will vary but may include:

Fear and Sadness: danger, wild, vile, foul, blackness, cold, shame, horror, trembled, loneliness, darkest, spitefulness, miserable, beastly, tears

Joy and Celebration: shining, golden, warmth, rich, jumping, clapping, laughing, leaping, beautiful, happy, romp, kisses

CD-104149 A Teacher's Guide to *The Lion, the Witch and the Wardrobe*

Page 46: Crossword

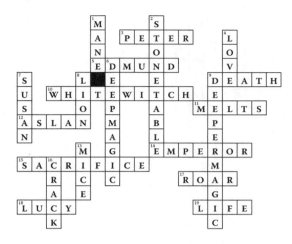

Page 47: Vocabulary and Comprehension

Vocabulary:
1. f
2. d
3. a
4. c
5. b
6. g
7. e

Comprehension:
1. Aslan comes to set the Witch's captives free.
2. He breathes on them.
3. Answers will vary.
4. Peter's army is losing because the Witch keeps turning them into stone.
5. Aslan pounces on the Witch.

Making the Story Your Own:

Answers will vary.

Page 49: Vocabulary and Comprehension

Vocabulary:
1. d
2. h
3. f
4. e
5. c
6. a
7. b
8. j
9. g
10. i

Comprehension:
1. He attacks the Witch and destroys her wand.
2. She uses the cordial to heal Edmund and the others who are wounded.
3. They destroy the Witch's army, make good laws, keep the peace.
4. They "talked in quite a different style now." They become King Peter the Magnificent, Susan the Gentle, King Edmund the Just, and Queen Lucy the Valiant.
5. They follow the White Stag through a thicket and out of the wardrobe.

Making the Story Your Own:

Answers will vary.

Page 51: Word Search

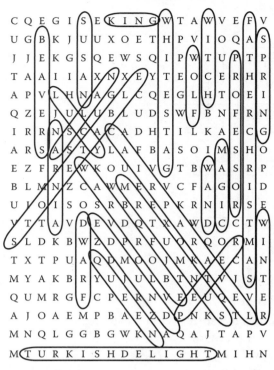

Page 52: Final Test (five points for each correct answer)

Matching: 1. d 2. a 3. b 4. e 5. c

True or False:

1. True
2. False—Edmund is mean and spiteful.
3. True
4. False—The Beavers are good creatures, on the side of Aslan against the Witch.
5. False—The Witch has the right to execute all traitors.
6. True
7. False—Aslan takes Edmund's place.
8. True
9. False—Aslan pounces on her in battle. (She's killed.)
10. True

Short Answer:

1. Always winter; never Christmas.
2. Aslan and/or the four Pevensie children (Peter, Susan, Edmund, and Lucy)
3. He's a traitor; he betrayed his own brother and sisters to the Witch.
4. Mr. and Mrs. Beaver
5. He lays down his own life in Edmund's place.

Essay: Answers will vary.

Bonus Question: Answers will vary.

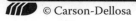
CD-104149 A Teacher's Guide to *The Lion, the Witch and the Wardrobe*